PIANO · VOCAL · GUITAR

THE **BIG BOOK** SECOND EDITION

CONTEMPORARY CHRISTIAN FAVORITES

ISBN 0-7935-4570-6

HAL•LEONARD®
CORPORATION

7777 W. BLUEMOUND RD. P.O. BOX 13819 MILWAUKEE, WI 53213

Visit Hal Leonard Online at
www.halleonard.com

CONTENTS

4   Abba (Father)   REBECCA ST. JAMES

11   Always Have, Always Will   AVALON

20   Angels   AMY GRANT

26   Chorus of Faith   MICHAEL CARD

32   Down on My Knees   SUSAN ASHTON

38   El Shaddai   AMY GRANT; MICHAEL CARD

44   Favorite Song of All   PHILLIPS, CRAIG & DEAN

52   Find a Way   AMY GRANT

62   Find Us Faithful   STEVE GREEN

57   Friends   MICHAEL W. SMITH

68   The Great Divide   POINT OF GRACE

75   Great Is the Lord   MICHAEL W. SMITH

78   He Walked a Mile   CLAY CROSSE

84   His Eyes   STEVEN CURTIS CHAPMAN

90   House That Mercy Built   POINT OF GRACE

96   I Will Be Here   STEVEN CURTIS CHAPMAN

102   I'll Be Believing   POINT OF GRACE

106   I'll Lead You Home   MICHAEL W. SMITH

114   In Christ Alone   MICHAEL ENGLISH

118   In Heaven's Eyes   SANDI PATTY

122   Jesus Freak   DC TALK

130   Just One   PHILLIPS, CRAIG & DEAN

135   Let Us Pray   STEVEN CURTIS CHAPMAN

142   A Little More   JENNIFER KNAPP

148   Love in Any Language SANDI PATTY

156   Love Will Be Our Home SANDI PATTY

164   A Maze of Grace AVALON

173   My Utmost for His Highest TWILA PARIS

178   Oh Lord, You're Beautiful KEITH GREEN

183   People Need the Lord STEVE GREEN

188   Pray REBECCA ST. JAMES

200   Revive Us, O Lord CARMAN

204   Run to You TWILA PARIS

212   Serve the Lord CARMAN

195   Shine on Us PHILLIPS, CRAIG & DEAN

224   Sing Your Praise to the Lord AMY GRANT; RICH MULLINS

230   Sometimes He Calms the Storm SCOTT KRIPPAYNE

240   Speechless STEVEN CURTIS CHAPMAN

237   There Is a Redeemer KEITH GREEN

254   This I Know MARGARET BECKER

262   This Love MARGARET BECKER

269   Thy Word AMY GRANT

274   To Know You NICHOLE NORDEMAN

282   Undivided FIRST CALL

287   Via Dolorosa SANDI PATTY

292   We Trust in the Name of the Lord Our God STEVE GREEN

297   Whatever You Ask STEVE CAMP

304   When It's Time to Go 4HIM

318   Where There Is Faith 4HIM

311   Wisdom TWILA PARIS

ABBA
(Father)

Words and Music by REBECCA ST. JAMES,
TEDD TJORNHOM and OTTO PRICE

Lyrics under staff:

I'm ___ feel-ing like the ea - gle that ris - es,
Run-ning in this race ___ 'til the fin - ish line,

They will soar like ea - gles. ____

ALWAYS HAVE, ALWAYS WILL

Words and Music by GRANT CUNNINGHAM,
TOBY McKEEHAN and NICK GONZALES

Part of me __ is the pro - di - gal, part of me __ is the oth - er broth - er.
I was born __ with a way - ward heart; still I live __ with the rest - less spir - it.

(Harmony 2nd time only)

You always will. will. _____

I'm gon - na keep trust - ing You. _____

I'm gon - na keep trust - ing You. _____

I see __ what You've seen me through. _____

I see __ what You've seen me ____ through. __

ANGELS

Words and Music by AMY GRANT, GARY CHAPMAN,
MICHAEL W. SMITH and BROWN BANNISTER

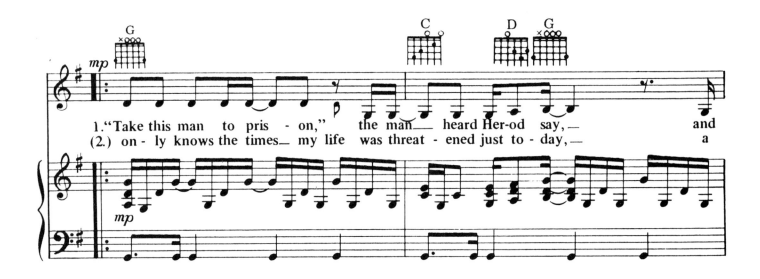

1. "Take this man to pris - on," the man heard Her-od say, — and
(2.) on - ly knows the times— my life was threat - ened just to - day, —

then four squads of sol - diers came— and car - ried him— a - way.   Chained
reck - less car ran out— of gas— be - fore it ran— my way.   Near

an-gels watch-ing ov - er me, an-gels watch-ing ov - er

me. _____ Though I nev-er see _ with hu - man eyes _ the hands _

____ that lead _ me home.

Repeat and fade

Optional ending

CHORUS OF FAITH

Words and Music by PHIL NAISH
and MICHAEL CARD

Sing it __ with your life, sing with _ your heart; Make mel - o - dy with the words of __ your mouth. But mind that _ you lis - ten, tell it __ to oth - ers.

DOWN ON MY KNEES

Words and Music by
WAYNE KIRKPATRICK

but I wal - low in ___ the mire of com - pla -
My de - sire's a - live and kick - ing, but my drive

- cen - cy, ___ that's when } I go down ___ on my knees. ___
___ is dead. ___ So,

Yeah, I want to

D.S. al Coda

CODA

You bear the weight of con - dem - na - tion, cleans - ing

EL SHADDAI

Words and Music by MICHAEL CARD
and JOHN THOMPSON

With much expression

With pedal

El Shad - dai, _____ El Shad - dai, _____ El El - yon _____ na A - do - nai, _____ age to age _____ you're still _____ the same, _____

FAVORITE SONG OF ALL

Words and Music by
DAN DEAN

FIND A WAY

Words and Music by MICHAEL W. SMITH
and AMY GRANT

FRIENDS

Words and Music by MICHAEL W. SMITH
and DEBORAH D. SMITH

FIND US FAITHFUL

Words and Music by
JON MOHR

THE GREAT DIVIDE

Words and Music by MATT HUESMANN
and GRANT CUNNINGHAM

Moderately

Si - lence,
faith - ful.
trying to fath - om the dis - tance,
On my own I'm un - a - ble.

look - ing out 'cross the can - yon
He found me hope - less, a - lone
carved by
and
sent a

70

GREAT IS THE LORD

Words and Music by MICHAEL W. SMITH
and DEBORAH D. SMITH

HE WALKED A MILE

Words and Music by
DAN MUCKALA

With much emotion ♩ = 69

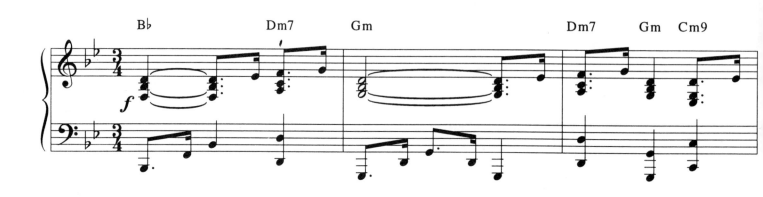

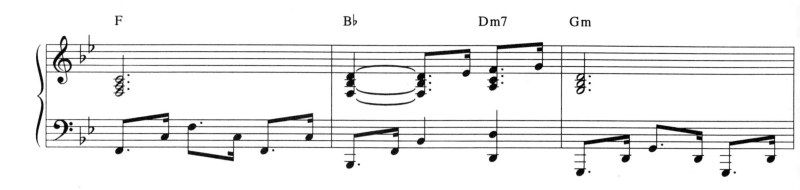

Be -

HIS EYES

Words and Music by STEVEN CURTIS CHAPMAN
and JAMES ISAAC ELLIOTT

1. Some -

times His eyes— were gen - tle and filled with laugh-ter,— and some-times they cried.
times His voice— comes call - ing like roll - ing thun - der,— or like driv - ing rain.

Some - times there was a fire— — of ho - ly an-ger— — in
And some - times His voice is qui - et and we start to won - der— if He

HOUSE THAT MERCY BUILT

Words and Music by MATT HUESMANN
and GRANT CUNNINGHAM

I WILL BE HERE

Words and Music by
STEVEN CURTIS CHAPMAN

To-mor-row morn-in' if you ___ wake up and the sun does not ___ ap-pear, ___
To-mor-row morn-in' if you ___ wake up and the fu-ture is ___ un-clear, ___

I, ___ I will be here.
I, ___ I will be here.

I'LL BE BELIEVING

Words and Music by GEOFFREY P. THURMAN
and BECKY THURMAN

When I'm a-walk-ing the straight and nar-row, some-times life throws a lit-tle curve. ___ If I

I'LL LEAD YOU HOME

Words and Music by MICHAEL W. SMITH
and WAYNE KIRKPATRICK

IN CHRIST ALONE

Words and Music by DON KOCH
and SHAWN CRAIG

IN HEAVEN'S EYES

Words and Music by
PHILL McHUGH

JESUS FREAK

Words and Music by TOBY McKEEHAN
and MARK HEIMERMANN

Peo - ple say I'm strange, does it___ make me a strang - er that my best friend was born___ in a man - ger?

in a man - ger?___

JUST ONE

Words and Music by CONNIE HARRINGTON
and JIM COOPER

LET US PRAY

Words and Music by
STEVEN CURTIS CHAPMAN

I hear you say __ your heart __ is ach - ing, you've got trou - ble in the mak -
So when we feel __ the Spir - it mov - ing, prompt-ing, prod-ding and be-hoov-

- ing, and you ask __ if I'll __ be pray-ing for __ you, please. __
- ing, there is no __ time to be los - ing, let us pray. __

A LITTLE MORE

Words and Music by
JENNIFER KNAPP

Turn Your eyes ____ from on this way. ____
For all the sin that lives in me,

I have proved ____ to live a das-tard-ly day. I ____
it took a nail to set ____ me free. Still, ____

hid my face ____ from the saints ____ and the an-
what I do ____ I ____ don't ____ wan-na do ____

LOVE IN ANY LANGUAGE

Words and Music by JOHN MAYS
and JON MOHR

* French   *** Russian (phonetic)

** Spanish   **** Hebrew

LOVE WILL BE OUR HOME

Words and Music by
STEVEN CURTIS CHAPMAN

A MAZE OF GRACE

Words and Music by GRANT CUNNINGHAM
and CHARLIE PEACOCK

MY UTMOST FOR HIS HIGHEST

Words and Music by
TWILA PARIS

With conviction ♩ = 80

1. When the Sav - ior came_ to earth, an - swer to the end - less fall,_ He be - came_ a man_ by
2. Stand - ing in_ this ho - ly place, let us all re - mem - ber here,_ cov - ered on - ly by_ His

OH LORD, YOU'RE BEAUTIFUL

Words and Music by
KEITH GREEN

PEOPLE NEED THE LORD

Words and Music by PHILL McHUGH
and GREG NELSON

head - ed who knows where.
shar - ing life with one who's lost.
On they go through
Through His love our

pri - vate pain,
hearts can feel
liv - ing fear to fear.
all the grief they bear.

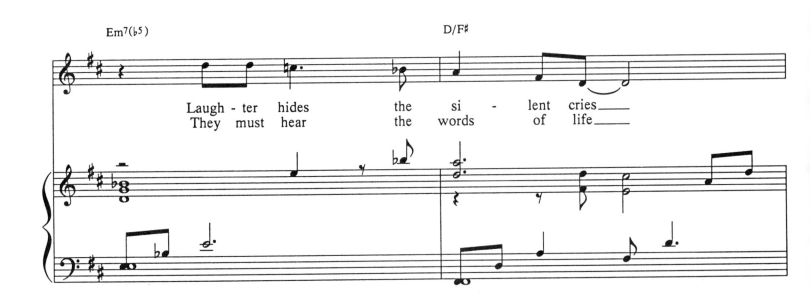

Laugh - ter hides the si - lent cries
They must hear the words of life

PRAY

Words and Music by REBECCA ST. JAMES,
MICHAEL QUINIAN and TEDD TJORNHOM

Slowly, very freely

Moderately fast

Je - sus, I am brok - en now. ___ Be - fore ___

* Vocal line written one octave higher than sung

Original key: Db major. This edition has been transposed down one half-step to be more playable.

SHINE ON US

Words and Music by MICHAEL W. SMITH
and DEBBIE SMITH

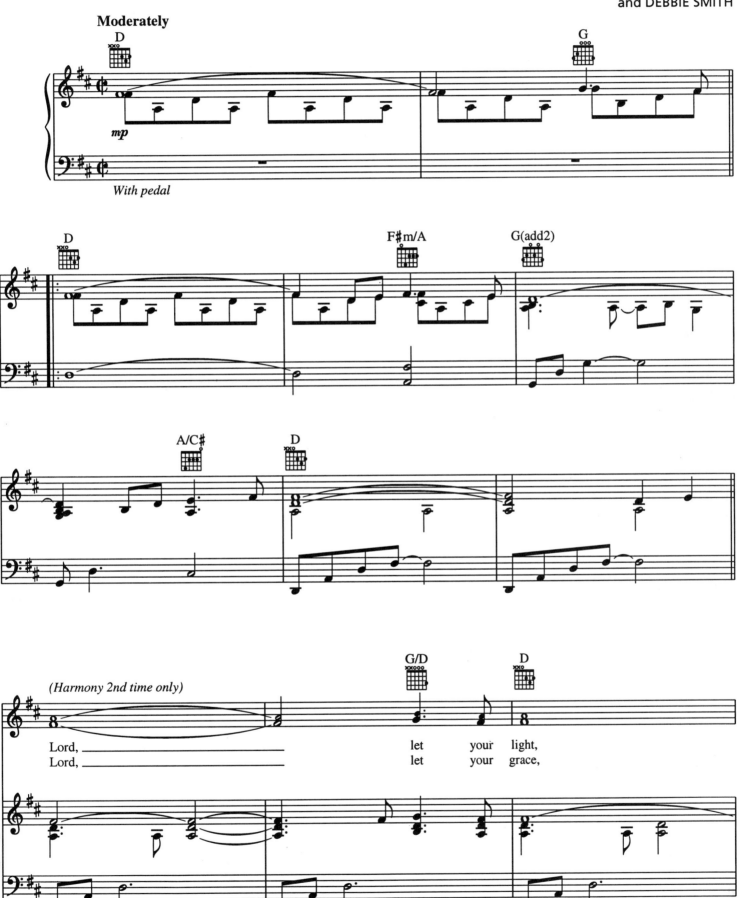

REVIVE US, O LORD

Words and Music by CARMAN
and STEVE CAMP

RUN TO YOU

Words and Music by
TWILA PARIS

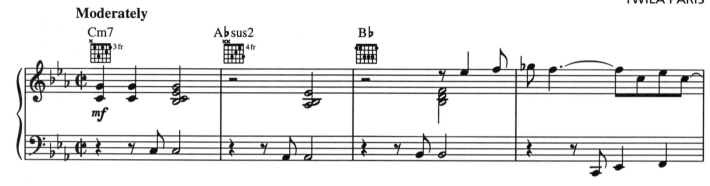

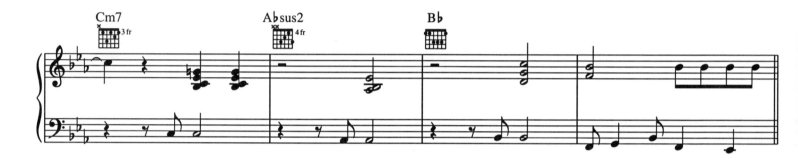

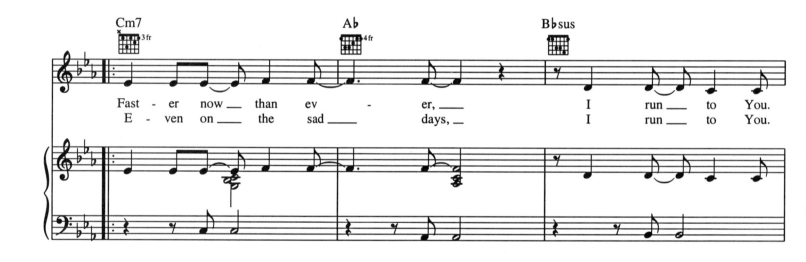

Fast- er now ___ than ev - er, ___ I run ___ to You.
E - ven on ___ the sad ___ days, ___ I run ___ to You.

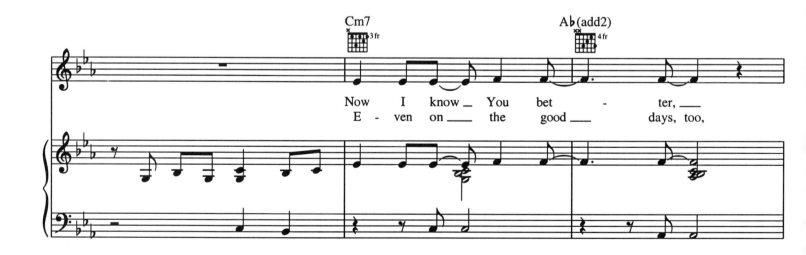

Now I know ___ You bet - ter, ___
E - ven on ___ the good ___ days, too,

Ooh, ___ I run ___ to You. ___

Ooh, ___ What else would ___ I do? ___ I run ___ to You. ___

SERVE THE LORD

Words and Music by
CARMAN

SING YOUR PRAISE TO THE LORD

Words and Music by
RICHARD MULLINS

Adapted from J.S.Bach's Fugue No.2 in C minor,WTC Vol.I

In a steady four, with excitement ♩ =88

226

sing, sing, — sing, let me hear ya now, sing, sing, — sing. ——

SOMETIMES HE CALMS THE STORM

Words and Music by KEVIN STOKES
and TONY WOOD

* *Background vocal sung 2nd time only.*

THERE IS A REDEEMER

Words and Music by
MELODY GREEN

1. There is a re - deem - er,
2.-4. *See additional lyrics*

Je - sus, God's own Son. _____

Additional Lyrics

2. **Jesus, my redeemer,**
   Name above all names.
   Precious Lamb of God, Messiah,
   Oh, for sinners slain. *(To Chorus)*

3. **When I stand in glory,**
   I will see His face,
   And there I'll serve my King forever
   In that holy place. *(To Chorus)*

4. **There is a redeemer,**
   Jesus, God's own Son.
   Precious Lamb of God, Messiah,
   Holy One. *(To Chorus)*

SPEECHLESS

Words and Music by STEVEN CURTIS CHAPMAN
and GEOFF MOORE

D.S. al Coda

THIS I KNOW

Words and Music by
MARGARET BECKER

THIS LOVE

Words and Music by MARGARET BECKER,
CHARLIE PEACOCK and KIP SUMMERS

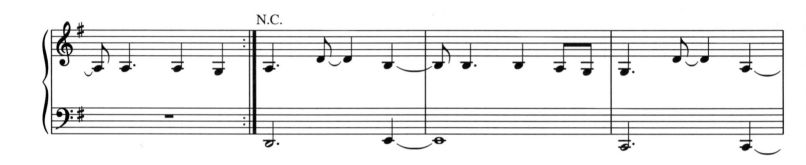

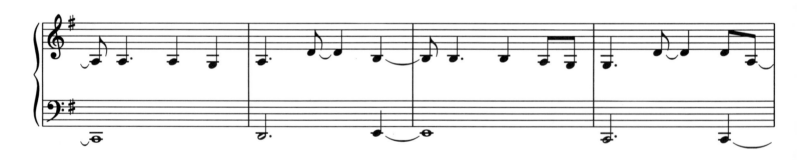

Not much heart left to break___
Not much rea - son to cry ___

THY WORD

Words and Music by MICHAEL W. SMITH
and AMY GRANT

TO KNOW YOU

Words and Music by NICHOLE NORDEMAN
and MARK HAMMOND

Moderately slow

It's well _ past mid-night and I'm a-wake _ with ques-tions that won't wait _ for day-light, sep-a-rat-ing fact _ from my i-mag-i-nar-y fic-tion on this shelf of my _ con-vic-tion. I

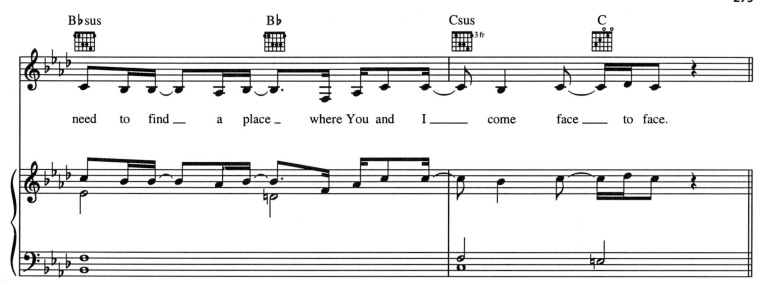

need to find a place where You and I come face to face.

Thom - as need-ed proof that You had real-ly ris-en
Nic - o-de-mus could not un-der-stand how You could

un - de-feat-ed. When he placed his fin-gers where the
tru - ly free us. He strug-gled with the im-age of a

nails once __ broke Your skin, __ did his faith fi - n'lly be - gin? ____ I've
grown man __ born a - gain. __ We might have been good friends, __ cuz

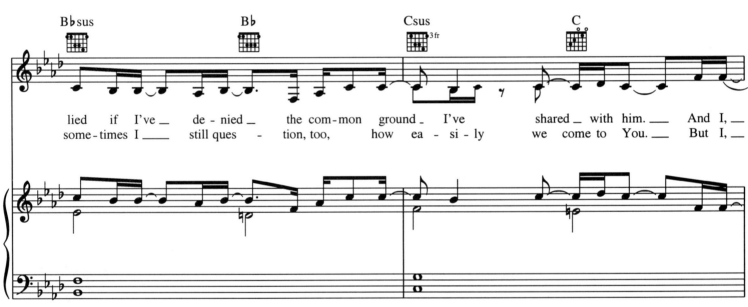

lied if I've __ de - nied __ the com-mon ground __ I've shared __ with him. __ And I, __
some-times I ____ still ques - tion, too, how ea - si - ly we come to You. __ But I, __

I real - ly want __ to know __ You. I

UNDIVIDED

Words and Music by
MELODIE TUNNEY

VIA DOLOROSA

Words and Music by BILLY SPRAGUE
and NILES BOROP

WE TRUST IN THE NAME OF THE LORD OUR GOD

Words and Music by
STEVEN CURTIS CHAPMAN

With energy

Some trust in chariots; we
Some trust in the work they do; we

trust in the name of the Lord our God.
trust in the name of the Lord our God.

Some trust in horses; we
'Cause by His grace all the work is through; we

trust in the name of the Lord our God.
trust in the name of the Lord our God.

We trust in the name of the Lord our

WHATEVER YOU ASK

Words and Music by PHILL McHUGH
and MICHELE WAGNER

WHEN IT'S TIME TO GO

Words and Music by JEFF SILVEY
and BILLY SIMON

Mystically

Noth-ing new __ in this __ old town, __ the sun comes up __ and heads __
Some years lat - er late __ one night __ he came in try'n __ to dry __

__ back down. __ Work-ing hard __ from dawn __ to dusk __ a - gain.
__ his eyes; __ he re - al - ized what he __ was born __ to do. __

WISDOM

Words and Music by
TWILA PARIS

Moderately slow groove

I see a mul - ti - tude_ of peo - ple,
There is a mo - ment of __ de - ci - sion,

WHERE THERE IS FAITH

Words and Music by
BILLY SIMON

I be - lieve __ in faith - ful - ness, __
There's a man __ a - cross __ the sea __

I be - lieve __ in giv - ing of __ my - self __
nev - er heard __ the sound __ of free - dom ring, __

for some - one __ else.
on - ly __ in __ his dreams. __

Where there _ is _____ faith there is ___ a

voice call - ing; _____ keep walk - ing, you're not ___ a -

lone in ___ this world. Where there _ is _____

faith there is ___ a peace like ___ a _____

Big Books of Music

Our "Big Books" feature big selections of popular titles under one cover, perfect for performing musicians, music aficionados or the serious hobbyist. All books are arranged for piano, voice, and guitar, and feature stay-open binding, so the books lie flat without breaking the spine.

BIG BOOK OF BALLADS
63 songs.
00310485 ....$19.95

**BIG BOOK OF
BIG BAND HITS**
84 songs.
00310701 ....$19.95

BIG BOOK OF BROADWAY
76 songs.
00311658 ....$19.95

**BIG BOOK OF
CHILDREN'S SONGS**
55 songs.
00359261 ....$12.95

**GREAT BIG BOOK OF
CHILDREN'S SONGS**
76 songs.
00310002 ....$14.95

**MIGHTY BIG BOOK OF
CHILDREN'S SONGS**
65 songs.
00310467 ....$14.95

**REALLY BIG BOOK OF
CHILDREN'S SONGS**
63 songs.
00310372 ....$15.95

**BIG BOOK OF
CHRISTMAS SONGS**
126 songs.
00311520 ....$19.95

**BIG BOOK OF
CLASSICAL MUSIC**
100 songs.
00310508 ....$19.95

**BIG BOOK OF
CONTEMPORARY
CHRISTIAN FAVORITES**
50 songs.
00310021 ....$19.95

**BIG BOOK OF
COUNTRY MUSIC**
64 songs.
00310188 ....$19.95

**BIG BOOK OF EARLY
ROCK N' ROLL**
99 songs.
00310398 ....$19.95

**BIG BOOK OF
GOSPEL SONGS**
100 songs.
00310604 ....$19.95

BIG BOOK OF HYMNS
125 hymns.
00310510 ....$17.95

BIG BOOK OF JAZZ
75 songs.
00311557 ....$19.95

**BIG BOOK OF
LATIN AMERICAN SONGS**
89 songs.
00311562 ....$19.95

**BIG BOOK OF LOVE AND
WEDDING SONGS**
80 songs.
00311567 ....$19.95

**BIG BOOK OF
MOVIE MUSIC**
72 songs.
00311582 ....$19.95

BIG BOOK OF NOSTALGIA
158 songs.
00310004 ....$19.95

**BIG BOOK OF
RHYTHM & BLUES**
67 songs.
00310169 ....$19.95

BIG BOOK OF ROCK
78 songs.
00311566 ....$19.95

BIG BOOK OF STANDARDS
86 songs.
00311667 ....$19.95

BIG BOOK OF SWING
84 songs.
00310359 ....$19.95

**BIG BOOK OF
TORCH SONGS**
75 songs.
00310561 ....$19.95

**BIG BOOK OF
TV THEME SONGS**
78 songs.
00310504 ....$19.95

The Finest Inspirational Music

Songbooks arranged for piano, voice, and guitar.

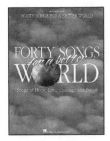

40 SONGS FOR A BETTER WORLD

40 songs with a message, including: All You Need Is Love • Bless The Beasts And Children • Colors Of The Wind • Everything Is Beautiful • He Ain't Heavy...He's My Brother • I Am Your Child • Love Can Build A Bridge • What A Wonderful World • What The World Needs Now Is Love • You've Got A Friend • and more.
00310096.............$15.95

BEST GOSPEL SONGS EVER

80 of the best-loved Gospel songs of all time, including: Amazing Grace • At Calvary • Because He Lives • Behold the Lamb • Daddy Sang Bass • Get All Excited • His Eye Is on the Sparrow • I Saw the Light • I'd Rather Have Jesus • I'll Fly Away • Just a Little Talk With Jesus • Mansion Over the Hilltop • My Tribute • Precious Lord, Take My Hand • and more.
00310503.............$19.95

CHRISTIAN CHILDREN'S SONGBOOK

Over 80 songs from Sunday School, including: Awesome God • The B-I-B-L-E • The Bible Tells Me So • Clap Your Hands • Day by Day • He's Got the Whole World in His Hands • I Am a C-H-R-I-S-T-I-A-N • I'm in the Lord's Army • If You're Happy (And You Know It) • Jesus Loves Me • Kum Ba Yah • Let There Be Peace on Earth • This Little Light of Mine • When the Saints Go Marching In • and more.
00310472.............$19.95

CHRISTIAN WEDDING SONGBOOK

Over 30 contemporary Christian wedding favorites, including: Bonded Together • Butterfly Kisses • Commitment Song • Flesh of My Flesh • Go There with You • Household of Faith • How Beautiful • Love Will Be Our Home • Make Us One • Parent's Prayer (Let Go of Two) • This Is the Day (A Wedding Song) • and more.
00310681.............$16.95

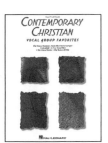

CONTEMPORARY CHRISTIAN VOCAL GROUP FAVORITES

15 songs, including: The Basics Of Life • A Few Good Men • The Great Divide • Undivided • and more.

00310019.............$10.95

CONTEMPORARY CHRISTIAN WEDDING SONGBOOK

30 appropriate songs for weddings, including: Household Of Faith • Love In Any Language • Love Will Be Our Home • Parents' Prayer • This Is Love • Where There Is Love • and more.
00310022.............$14.95

COUNTRY/GOSPEL U.S.A.

50 songs written for piano/guitar/four-part vocal. Highlights: An American Trilogy • Daddy Sang Bass • He Set Me Free • I Saw The Light • I'll Meet You In The Morning • Kum Ba Yah • Mansion Over The Hilltop • Love Lifted Me • Turn Your Radio On • When The Saints Go Marching In • many more.
00240139.............$9.95

FAVORITE HYMNS

An outstanding collection of 71 all-time favorites, including: Abide With Me • Amazing Grace • Ave Maria • Bringing In The Sheaves • Christ The Lord Is Risen Today • Crown Him With Many Crowns • Faith Of Our Fathers • He's Got The Whole World In His Hands • In The Sweet By And By • Jesus Loves Me! • Just A Closer Walk With Thee • Kum Ba Yah • A Mighty Fortress Is Our God • Onward Christian Soldiers • Rock Of Ages • Swing Low, Sweet Chariot • Were You There? • and many more!
00490436.............$12.95

GREAT HYMNS TREASURY

A comprehensive collection of 70 favorites: Close To Thee • Footsteps Of Jesus • Amazing Grace • At The Cross • Blessed Assurance • Blest Be The Tie That Binds • Church In The Wildwood • The Church's One Foundation • God Of Our Fathers • His Eye Is On The Sparrow • How Firm A Foundation • I Love To Tell The Story • In The Garden • It Is Well With My Soul • Just A Closer Walk With Thee • Just As I Am • Nearer My God, To Thee • Now That We All Our God • The Old Rugged Cross • The Lily Of The Valley • We're Marching To Zion • Were You There? • What A Friend We Have In Jesus • When I Survey The Wondrous Cross • and more.
00310167.............$12.95

THE NEW YOUNG MESSIAH

Matching folio to the album featuring today's top contemporary Christian artists performing a modern rendition of Handel's *Messiah*. Features Sandi Patty, Steven Curtis Chapman, Larnelle Harris, and others.
00310006.............$16.95

OUR GOD REIGNS

A collection of over 70 songs of praise and worship, including: El Shaddai • Find Us Faithful • His Eyes • Holy Ground • How Majestic Is Your Name • Proclaim The Glory Of The Lord • Sing Your Praise To The Lord • Thy Word • and more.
00311695.............$17.95

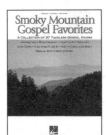

SMOKY MOUNTAIN GOSPEL FAVORITES

37 favorites, including: Amazing Grace • At Calvary • At The Cross • Blessed Assurance • Church In The Wildwood• I Love To Tell The Story • In The Garden • In The Sweet By And By • The Old Rugged Cross • Rock Of Ages • Shall We Gather At The River • Softly And Tenderly • Tell It To Jesus • Wayfaring Stranger • We're Marching To Zion • What A Friend We Have In Jesus • When The Roll Is Called Up Yonder • When We All Get to Heaven • and more.
00310161.............$8.95

ULTIMATE GOSPEL – 100 SONGS OF DEVOTION

Includes: El Shaddai • His Eye Is On The Sparrow • How Great Thou Art • Just A Closer Walk With Thee • Lead Me, Guide Me • (There'll Be) Peace In The Valley (For Me) • Precious Lord, Take My Hand • Wings Of A Dove • more.

00241009.............$19.95

Contemporary Christian Folios

HEAVEN AND EARTH

Matching folio to the album, featuring: As We Wait • Heaven and Earth • Jesus, Hail the Lamb • River of Life • and more.
00306335
P/V/G
$14.95

TWILA PARIS – TRUE NORTH

Matching folio with 11 songs, including: Could You Believe • Delight My Heart • I Choose Grace • True North • and more.
00306330
P/V/G
$14.95

STEVEN CURTIS CHAPMAN – GREATEST HITS

14 of his best: The Great Adventure • Heaven in the Real World • His Eyes • His Strength Is Perfect • Lord of the Dance • No Better Place • Not Home Yet • The Walk • more.
00306196
P/V/G
$16.95

REBECCA ST. JAMES ~ PRAY

Includes 11 songs from her album: Be Thou My Vision • Come Quickly Lord • Give Myself Away • Hold Me Jesus • I'll Carry You • Lord You're Beautiful • Love to Love You • Mirror • OK • Omega • Peace • Pray.
00306268
P/V/G
$14.95

JANET PASCHAL – SONGS FOR A LIFETIME

12 favorite songs from this Contemporary Christian artist, including: Been Through Enough • Faithful Father • God Will Make a Way • I Am Not Ashamed • and more.
00306328
P/V/G
$14.95

TWILA PARIS – PERENNIAL

Matching folio to this contemporary Christian artist's album, including the songs: Amazing Grace • Be Thou My Vision • Faithful Men • Father, We are Here • Perennial • and more.
00306232
P/V/G
$14.95

AVALON – IN A DIFFERENT LIGHT

All 11 songs from this talented contemporary Christian vocal quartet's 1999 release: Always Have, Always Will • Can't Live a Day • First Love • Hide My Soul • I'm Speechless • If My People Pray • In a Different Light • In Not Of • Let Your Love • Only for the Weak • Take You at Your Word.
00306295
P/V/G
$14.95

STEVE GREEN – MORNING LIGHT

Songs to Awaken the Dawn
This songbook includes 12 songs from this popular contemporary Christian artist's album, including: All That You Say • Doxology • I Offer Myself • I Will Awaken the Dawn • Listen • Lord of the Dawn • Morning Has Broken • Morning Star • Selah • and more.
00306313
P/V/G
$14.95

DELIRIOUS? – KING OF FOOLS

Includes all of the songs from their latest album: All the Way • August 30th • Deeper • Hands of Kindness • History Maker • King of Fools • King or Cripple • Louder Than the Radio • Promise • Revival Town • Sanctify • What a Friend • White Ribbon Day.
00306254
P/V/G
$16.95

JENNIFER KNAPP – KANSAS

The matching folio to this Dove Award-winning contemporary Christian folk-rocker's Gotee Records release features 11 songs: Faithful to Me • His Grace Is Sufficient • Hold Me Now • In the Name • Undo Me • Visions • Whole Again. Includes great photos and playing notes.
00306324
P/V/G
$12.95

STEVEN CURTIS CHAPMAN – SPEECHLESS

13 songs from the latest by Steven Curtis Chapman, who in his career has won 38 Dove Awards and 3 Grammies. Includes: Be Still and Know • The Change • Dive • Fingerprints of God • Great Expectations • I Do Believe • The Invitation • Whatever • With Hope.
00306316
P/V/G
$14.95

FOR MORE INFORMATION, SEE YOUR LOCAL MUSIC DEALER, OR WRITE TO:

HAL•LEONARD® CORPORATION

7777 W. BLUEMOUND RD. P.O. BOX 13819 MILWAUKEE, WI 53213

For a complete listing of the products we have available.
Visit Hal Leonard Online at
www.halleonard.com

Prices, contents & availability subject to change without notice.

0401